TAYLOR MANNING

Start Delegating Now

Practical and Proven Strategies to Go from Overwhelmed to Owning It

Copyright © 2024 by Taylor Manning

All rights reserved. No part of this publication may be reproduced, stored or transmitted in any form or by any means, electronic, mechanical, photocopying, recording, scanning, or otherwise without written permission from the publisher. It is illegal to copy this book, post it to a website, or distribute it by any other means without permission.

First edition

This book was professionally typeset on Reedsy.
Find out more at reedsy.com

Contents

1 Introduction — 1
2 Chapter 1: Understanding the Fundamentals of Delegation — 3
3 Chapter 2: Building a Delegation-Friendly Culture — 6
4 Chapter 3: Identifying Delegation Opportunities — 10
5 Chapter 4: The Delegation Process — 17
6 Chapter 5: Diagnosing Delegation Failures — 22
7 Chapter 6: Developing Your Team through Delegation — 28
8 Chapter 7: Measuring the Impact of Delegation — 34
9 Conclusion — 38

1

Introduction

Let's be real here—being a manager is no joke. You've got a team to lead, deadlines to hit, and probably a million other things on your plate. And if you're like most new managers, you're probably wondering how the heck you're supposed to get it all done without working 24/7.

That's where the art of delegation comes in. Delegation is like a superpower for managers—it's the ability to empower your team members to take on tasks and responsibilities, freeing up your time and energy to focus on the big-picture stuff.

Now, I know what you might be thinking: "But won't delegating just create more work for me? What if they screw it up?" Trust me, I've been there. Delegation can seem scary, especially when you're just starting as a manager. But here's the thing—done right, delegation is a game-changer.

Think about it: when you delegate effectively, you're not just offloading tasks; you're developing your team's skills and giving them opportunities to grow. Plus, you're setting yourself up for success by building a team that can handle more and more responsibilities over time. It's a win-win situation.

But delegation isn't just about throwing tasks over the fence and hoping for the best. It's an art form that requires careful planning, communication, and trust-building. That's what this book is all about—equipping you with the tools and strategies you need to become a delegation ninja.

We'll cover everything from identifying the right tasks to delegate to fostering a culture of accountability and ownership to overcoming your self-sabotaging neuroses and letting go of that death grip on control.

So buckle up, my friend. We're about to embark on a journey towards becoming a delegation master. By the end of this book, you'll be delegating like a pro, freeing up your time and energy to focus on the things that matter—like strategizing, innovating, and leading your team to new heights of awesomeness.

Are you ready to unlock the power of delegation? Let's do this!

2

Chapter 1: Understanding the Fundamentals of Delegation

You can't master delegation without first understanding what it means. In this chapter, we're going to break it down and separate fact from fiction. Get ready to confront some common delegation myths and misconceptions that might be holding you back. And we'll take an honest look at your current delegation skills (or lack thereof) so you know exactly where you're starting from. Saddle up, rookie — this is Delegation 101.

Newsflash: being a rockstar manager or leader doesn't give you superpowers. No matter how talented, experienced, or caffeinated you are, there's a hard limit to how much you can take on solo. But as the old saying goes, *if you want something done right, you have to do it yourself...* Right? Not quite. That's just a recipe for burnout and disaster.

Because here's the thing: as our organizations continue to grow and evolve, we quickly learn that we simply can't do it all ourselves. No matter how tempting it might be, it's just not sustainable—or smart—to try and white-knuckle every single task and responsibility.

That's where delegation comes in. But I know what you're thinking: "Woah, hang on there, partner. Delegation? Isn't that just code for 'dumping my work on someone else'? Am I setting myself up for chaos?"

I hear you. We've all made the same justifications: "It'll take me more time to explain how to do this than if I just did it myself." "The more I delegate, the greater the risk that something will go wrong." Or, maybe you've tried delegating in the past, only for it to go belly up. "Delegating just sets me up for conflict and disappointment—and I'll probably end up having to do it myself anyway."

Those worries and fears are totally normal—and valid! Delegation can indeed be messy, frustrating, and fraught with challenges. It's not just about tossing tasks over the cubicle wall and hoping for the best.

But see, learning how to properly delegate isn't just some nice-to-have skill. It's an absolute must if you want to level up as a leader and take your team to new heights. Why? Because delegation is the ultimate force multiplier.

Think about it: you have limits on your time, energy, and bandwidth. But by delegating effectively, you can harness the collective strengths and efforts of your entire team. You're not just offloading tasks—you're empowering others to contribute, develop new skills, and take ownership.

Now, I'm not going to lie to you. Learning to be a delegation ninja is no walk in the park. It takes time, effort, and a whole lot of struggle. As Sam Chand puts it, "A leader will only grow to the threshold of his pain." Embracing delegation and all the messy realities that come with it is going to push your limits and stretch you in some uncomfortable ways.

But the more pain and struggle you can handle, the higher you'll go as

CHAPTER 1: UNDERSTANDING THE FUNDAMENTALS OF DELEGATION

a leader. By learning to delegate and avoiding the hair-pulling missteps, you'll widen your base of support and expand your horizons in ways you can't imagine. It's like going from a one-man lemonade stand to a lemonade franchise in multiple locations (albeit with a few spilled pitchers and sticky floors along the way).

Again, this won't be easy. Delegation is like a full-body workout for managers: it'll make you sweat, curse under your breath, and maybe even shed a few tears of frustration (or at least get a little misty-eyed). But stick with me, keep an open mind, and put in the work, and I promise the payoff will be worth it.

Because mastering delegation isn't about memorizing some checklist or rigid set of rules. It's about building the mindset, habits, and structures to empower your team in a way that drives real results and unlocks new levels of leadership. It's about turning delegation from some dreaded chore into a core strength and competitive advantage.

You'll go from delegation doubter and control freak to a bona fide empowerment master. You'll turn those "do it myself" thoughts into a distant memory, replaced by a team of skilled, capable problem-solvers working together like a well-oiled machine. You'll trade in your lemonade stand for the big leagues—all thanks to your newfound delegation kung-fu.

So what do you say? Are you ready to embrace the struggle and start building your delegation muscles? If so, grab yourself a pen, a notebook, and a supersized lemonade (you'll need the energy). We're about to go from delegation disaster to delegation boss.

3

Chapter 2: Building a Delegation-Friendly Culture

> *Delegation doesn't happen in a vacuum. You need to cultivate the right environment for it to thrive. Here's where we'll dive into fostering a culture of trust, open communication, and accountability within your team. Because let's face it, trying to delegate without those key ingredients is like trying to bake a cake without eggs—it just ain't gonna rise, my friend. Get ready to roll up your sleeves and start building a delegation-friendly foundation.*

Alright, delegation padawans—let's get down to business. First off, having raw talent on your team isn't enough to make delegation work. Don't get me wrong, skilled team members are a huge asset. But if you want to unlock the full potential of delegation, you need an environment that's primed and ready for it. You need a delegation-friendly **culture**.

Now, I can already hear the skeptics out there: "Culture? What is

CHAPTER 2: BUILDING A DELEGATION-FRIENDLY CULTURE

this, some kind of corporate karma circle?" Let me break it down for you: culture is the shared values, behaviors, and unwritten rules that shape how work actually gets done in your team or organization. It's the difference between delegation feeling like a natural process... or feeling like you're trying to swim upstream through a raging river of chaos and mistrust.

Unfortunately, you can't just delegate willy-nilly to anyone and expect it to work seamlessly. Both you as the delegating leader and the person you're delegating to have to demonstrate a certain level of maturity for this whole shebang to work. I'm talking about the real kind of maturity—not the "I ate my vegetables and didn't yell at the waitress" kind.

When I say maturity, I mean your team members need to know their limitations and when to ask for help. They need to have the actual competence and skills not only to do the task but to do it in the right way, at the right time. And perhaps most importantly, they need to have a track record of diligence and integrity, consistently delivering excellence and then working hard to maintain it.

On your end as the delegator, you need to walk the talk and set the tone for your team's culture. You need to model the kind of integrity, work ethic, and speed that you want your delegates to embody. Because culture is like a garden—if you don't tend to it and nurture the right behaviors, you'll be overrun with weeds before you know it.

How do you know if you're nurturing the right environment? Here are some key questions to reflect on as you're building (or rebooting) a truly delegation-friendly culture:

1. Do my people understand why what we do is important and how it fits into the bigger picture? You can't expect bought-in delegation if people are just going through the motions without context.
2. Are my expectations crystal-freaking-clear, or are they more like a

hazy, cloudy mess? Unclear expectations are a culture killer.
3. Am I actually holding people accountable for their performance, or just letting things slide? You can't delegate and then check out.
4. Do I make an active effort to identify and remove barriers that make their jobs harder than they need to be? Delegation doesn't work if your team is constantly hitting roadblocks.
5. Am I giving my team the freedom, autonomy, and psychological safety required to learn, grow, and truly deliver? Micromanaging = anti-delegation.
6. How am I being complicit in enabling the current situation or culture that I keep complaining about? Sometimes you have to look in the mirror.

The answers to those questions can be brutal—but self-awareness is key. You can't just slap some "We Have a Delegation Culture!" posters up on the wall and call it a day. It takes real work to create an environment where delegation is seen as normal, expected, and supported.

That means fostering a foundation of trust and open communication. Your team needs to feel safe to ask questions, raise concerns, and occasionally fail without fear of getting chewed out or fired. You need to cultivate a mentality of accountability and ownership, where people take pride in seeing delegated tasks through to completion. Perhaps most importantly, you need to recognize and celebrate delegation wins—those little victories when a task gets handed off smoothly and your delegate knocks it out of the park.

Now, building that kind of culture won't happen overnight. It's a constant work in progress, filled with plenty of tough conversations, and moments where you wonder if it's all worth it. There will be times when delegation feels like an uphill battle against politics, bureaucracy, and good old-fashioned pettiness.

CHAPTER 2: BUILDING A DELEGATION-FRIENDLY CULTURE

But I guarantee you this: the more you prioritize shaping a delegation-friendly culture, the more delegation will become like second nature for you and your team. What starts as a clunky, awkward process, will gradually evolve into a well-choreographed dance, with tasks and responsibilities seamlessly flowing between you and your skilled, empowered team members.

You'll go from pushing delegation through sheer force of will to having it become just part of how you all operate. You'll trade in a culture of chaos and confusion for one of clarity, accountability, and mutual respect. And when that culture is firmly rooted, you'll find delegation is not only easier—it becomes a key part of your competitive advantage as a team.

So get ready to get a little tough on yourself. Reflect on those key questions, identify the cultural roadblocks, and start planting the seeds for a thriving delegation ecosystem. It won't be easy, and there will be plenty of times when you feel like ripping your hair out (or offering to trade your delegate for a new team member). But stick with it, keep your eyes on the prize, and you'll reap the rewards of a well-oiled delegation machine for years to come.

4

Chapter 3: Identifying Delegation Opportunities

Okay, you've got the basics down and your team is primed for delegation success. Now it's time to figure out what the heck you should be delegating. We'll go through a process for assessing your responsibilities, determining which tasks are delegation-worthy, and matching those bad boys up with the right team members. No more randomly tossing tasks over the cubicle wall—it's time for a strategic approach.

Now we've covered the fundamentals of delegation and laid the groundwork for a real delegation-friendly culture. But now we're getting to the meat of the matter: figuring out what the heck you should be delegating in the first place.

Because let's be honest, simply chucking random tasks over the cubicle wall at your team like you're redecorating your office with a fresh new paper snowstorm isn't going to cut it. That's a one-way ticket to the

CHAPTER 3: IDENTIFYING DELEGATION OPPORTUNITIES

delegation disaster zone.

No, if you want to be a true delegation master, you need to be strategic and intentional about what you hand off—and to whom. You need to take a good hard look at how you're spending your time and identify the high-leverage, high-impact activities that only you can (or should) be doing as the leader.

Now, I already know what some of you are thinking: "But I'm completely swamped all the time! How am I supposed to find the bandwidth to even think about delegating when I can barely keep my head above water?"

Fair point, my perpetually overwhelmed friend. That's why we need to start with a little exercise I like to call the *Time Audit*.

Here's how it works: for one typical week, you're going to track how you're spending your time in 30-minute increments. Yep, all of it—no cheating! Write down exactly what you're doing every half hour, from clearing out those 500 unread emails to hitting up your 10th coffee refill of the day.

Once you have that raw data truthfully documented (and I mean truthfully—no fudging the Netflix hours), you'll go through and rank each activity based on its impact on your core goals and priorities using this simple five-tier system:

Tier 1: Mission-critical tasks that only you can do and drive massive impact

Tier 2: Very important, strategic tasks that are huge leverage for you

Tier 3: Meaningful tasks that contribute to goals but aren't necessarily vital

Tier 4: Lower priority tasks initiated by others that don't drive high impact

Tier 5: Total and complete time-wasters (you know the ones!)

To help you categorize those activities, here are some additional questions to reflect on:

- Where is your time most valuable as the leader? What tasks simply can't be done (or done well) by anyone else?
- Which tasks will create the biggest impact for your team/organization if you devote more time to them?
- What are you honestly just not very good at or skilled in? Those could be prime delegation opportunities.
- What tasks do you absolutely loathe and dread doing? You're probably not the best person for those.

CHAPTER 3: IDENTIFYING DELEGATION OPPORTUNITIES

TIME	MONDAY	TUESDAY	WEDNESDAY	THURSDAY	FRIDAY
08.00					
08.30					
09.00					
09.30					
10.00					
10.30					
11.00					
11.30					
12.00					
12.30					
13.00					
13.30					
14.00					
14.30					
15.00					
15.30					
16.00					
16.30					
17.00					
17.30					
18.00					
18.30					

Once you have everything mapped out into those five tiers, it's time for the fun part: deciding how to handle each tier. You've got three main options:

Option 1: **Eliminate**

This one is pretty straightforward: any tasks that made it into your Tier 5 "Total Waste of Time" category should be ruthlessly eliminated from your schedule altogether. Do not pass go, do not collect $200—just get rid of them. You're the leader, damn it! You don't have time for busywork that doesn't matter.

Option 2: **Automate**

For those tasks in Tiers 3 and 4 that do need to get done but aren't great uses of your time, look for ways to automate or streamline them. Maybe it's investing in some snazzy new software or just getting a little script-kiddie with some simple code. The goal is to make those low-leverage tasks as painless and effortless as possible.

Option 3: **Delegate**

This is where the real magic happens. Take a good long look at your Tier 1 and Tier 2 activities—the ones that are hugely important and massively impactful but maybe aren't solely your responsibility. Which of those could be delegated to capable team members? Match each task to the person who is best suited and positioned to take it on.

But heads up! Don't just dump those tasks on some unsuspecting victim and call it a day. We'll dive much deeper into the art of effective delegation in later chapters. But at a high level, you need to properly train your delegates, set them up for success with the right context and resources, and provide clear expectations and accountability. Delegation isn't a magic wand—it's a skill that requires effort on both sides.

Now, as you go through this exercise of categorizing and handling your tasks, you might start to feel a little twinge of sadness about some of those Tier 5 time-sucks you're eliminating or Tier 4 distractions you're automating away. Maybe you secretly loved spiraling down those Reddit rabbit holes or spending hours tinkering with that spam filter script.

CHAPTER 3: IDENTIFYING DELEGATION OPPORTUNITIES

If so, I've got some tough love for you: you need to get over it, buttercup.

The best people in any field get 100% of the work done in just 80% of the time. That's what makes them so ridiculously effective and impactful. And you know what they do with that extra 20% of their time? They don't fritter it away on trivial busywork or distractions. They use it to push boundaries, explore new ideas, and find those little areas of huge potential impact that everyone else is too buried or blind to see.

That's the power of relentless prioritization and focus. Of being brutally honest about where you're spending your time and proactively redirecting it towards only the highest-leverage activities through elimination, automation, and delegation.

Will it be hard at first? Of course! Breaking old habits and freeing up brain cycles that were once devoted to meaningless tasks is tough. But trust me, as you start implementing the tactics from this time audit exercise, you'll quickly start to see the payoff.

You'll notice your days feeling less frenetic and overwhelming. You'll start spotting opportunities for big wins that were previously hidden under piles of trivial nonsense. You'll even start to enjoy the feeling of control and clarity that comes from a finely-tuned schedule packed with nothing but high-impact work.

And perhaps most importantly, you'll have cleared the pathway to allow delegation to truly become a core part of how you operate. You can't effectively delegate to your team if you're constantly drowning in busywork yourself. But once you've drained that swamp of minutiae through elimination and automation? Delegation will start to feel like a release valve rather than another chore on your never-ending to-do list.

So go ahead—carve out some distraction-free time, track your weekly schedule with ruthless honesty, and start making some tough triage decisions about where you spend your precious time and energy. It won't be easy, but few massively impactful things ever are.

Stick with it, keep that vision of focused, high-leverage leadership in mind, and pretty soon delegating will shift from being a frantic stopgap to an integral part of how you drive results. You'll trade in those chaos-filled days of trying desperately to do it all for the cool confidence that comes from uplifting and empowering your team.

It all starts with consistently identifying what's worth doing in the first place—and having the guts to cut out everything else. Who's ready to start slashing and burning their way to a delegation-primed schedule?

5

Chapter 4: The Delegation Process

This is where the rubber meets the road. We're laying out a step-by-step guide for effectively delegating tasks, from preparation to follow-up. You'll learn how to set clear objectives, provide context, and manage expectations like a boss. We'll also cover techniques for communicating throughout the process and giving feedback that helps your team members grow. Get ready to become a delegation pro.

Now we've reached the main event. You've absorbed the fundamentals of delegation, you've put in the hard work of building a delegation-friendly culture, and you've got a sharp eye for identifying the right opportunities to hand off tasks and responsibilities.

But now we're getting down to brass tacks: the actual nuts and bolts of how to delegate effectively. Because you can have all the right intentions and a sublime grasp of the philosophy, but if you don't nail the execution, it's all for naught.

As management G.O.A.T. Peter Drucker once said, "The most important decision a leader makes is: who does what." By deciding who on your team tackles which pieces of work, you're essentially putting together a system by which things actually get done.

Effective delegation is all about intentionally designing and communicating that system in a crystal clear, empowering way. It's about defining who does what, when, and how with total clarity. No more awkward shoulder taps or sloppy passes in the hallway—we're talking full responsibility for conveying the idea, the gaps, the rationale, and the payoff.

But before we get too far into the weeds, let's take a step back: why does delegating well even matter all that much? Can't you just slap some tasks on a project management app and call it a day?

Sure, you could do that. But I guarantee that that lackluster approach will actively undermine all the great work you've done so far to build an environment primed for delegation success. It'll erode trust, fuel frustration, and give your team a convenient excuse to avoid taking true ownership and accountability.

No, if you want to reap the full benefits of leveraging your team through delegation, you need to approach it with the same level of care, preparation, and communication that you'd put into any other mission-critical process.

So let's walk through a simple framework for what you need to provide when delegating any task or responsibility:

Description

This one seems obvious, but you'd be amazed how often it gets botched. When kicking off a delegation scenario, you need to start with a crisp, active description that clearly answers the "what" and the "when." Avoid vague phrasing and fluffy concepts—use punchy action verbs and be explicit about deliverables and deadlines.

CHAPTER 4: THE DELEGATION PROCESS

Rationale

This part answers the pivotal "why"—as in, "Why are we doing this in the first place?" You need to provide crucial context around the bigger-picture objectives and reasons for the task. Don't just treat your delegates like mindless order-takers; help them understand the meaning and importance behind the work.

Parameters

Every delegation scenario has certain boundaries and guardrails. Maybe it's budgetary constraints, immovable deadlines, a fixed pool of resources to draw from, or key milestones that have to be hit along the way. Lay out those parameters from the jump so your team isn't left guessing or going rogue later.

Vision

This one is absolutely critical: you need to take the time to clearly define and articulate what a "win" actually looks like for the task or project at hand. Don't just assume your delegate has the same definition of success rattling around in their head. Spell it out in vivid detail so they know exactly what they're aiming for.

Input

This is where you clearly spell out what your level of involvement will be based on the specific scenario and the skill level of your delegate. In this framework, there are five potential "input" levels you can opt for, each with a clear delineation of decision-making authority.

These five levels are:

Level 1. ***Instruction***

This is for true delegating 101 scenarios where you need to train your delegate on the exact process. You'll demonstrate the task, watch them mirror it back, and provide detailed, step-by-step directions.

Level 2. ***Investigation***

Cut your delegate a little more slack by having them research or study up on the task, then report back with their findings and questions.

You're available as a hands-on resource.

Level 3. *Informed Progress*

Now we're cooking with gas! At this level, your delegate will do their own research, outline potential options and approaches, and recommend a path forward for your approval before executing.

Level 4. *Informed Results*

Here, you're taking more of a hands-off approach. Your delegate has the autonomy to dive in, make key decisions, and keep you updated primarily on status, milestones, and final results, rather than all the nitty-gritty details.

Level 5. *Ownership*

At this level, you're firmly in "trust the process" mode. Provide the high-level desired outcome, then get out of the way and let your delegate own the planning, execution, and decision-making, from start to finish.

So how do you determine which level to opt for? It's all about tailoring the specifics for the situation and the individual.

For total newbies still finding their feet, you'll want to start with more hand-holding through Levels 1 and 2 of intensive coaching and shadowing. As their competence, ownership, and track record of success grows over time, you can gradually ratchet up the autonomy through Levels 3 and 4.

And for those elite-level delegates who've proven they can crush it with little oversight? Grant Level 5 ownership, set the high-level vision, and get the heck out of the way so they can work their magic.

The key thing to understand is that effective delegation isn't a rigid, one-size-fits-all process. It's a living, dynamic exchange that requires constantly calibrating your level of input based on your team's capabilities and needs in any given scenario.

Maybe that requires you to break out the pedagogical skills and walk a fresh-faced teammate through a process step-by-tedious-step. Or perhaps it calls for a much lighter touch of simply articulating the

CHAPTER 4: THE DELEGATION PROCESS

desired outcomes and giving them the keys to get there.

But no matter what level of input and oversight you opt for, the constants are:

1. Providing a crystal clear delineation of responsibilities upfront
2. Aligning on the "why" behind the work
3. Establishing clear boundaries and constraints
4. Painting a vivid picture of what "done" or "success" looks like
5. Committing to be as hands-on or hands-off as the situation demands

If you commit to walking through those five delegation steps with diligence and care, you'll immediately elevate your delegation game. You'll bypass the whirlpools of confusion and misalignment that plague so many half-hearted hand-off attempts. And your team, in turn, will be empowered to take on new challenges and responsibilities with enthusiasm instead of trepidation.

It's a delicate dance of enabling without bottlenecking, guidance without micromanagement, and trust paired with verification. But when you get the balance right and assemble all those pieces with intentionality? That's when delegating goes from an anxiety-inducing chore to a confidence-inspiring system for multiplying your team's impact.

It's a step-by-step journey from delegation disaster to a slam dunk. It'll take practice, patience, and a willingness to course-correct when things go sideways (which they inevitably will at some point). But pull it off consistently, and you'll have unlocked one of the most powerful skills in a leader's arsenal.

Get ready for impact, y'all. The delegation mastery journey continues!

6

Chapter 5: Diagnosing Delegation Failures

Delegation isn't all rainbows and unicorns. There are very real fears, challenges, and bad habits that can sabotage your efforts. In this chapter, we'll confront those delegation demons head-on, from your need for control to a lack of trust in your team. You'll figure out where you're going wrong, and how to go about letting go of the reins (gradually, of course—we don't want anyone getting thrown from the horse).

We've covered a ton of ground so far on this delegation mastery journey. You've absorbed the fundamentals, shaped an environment primed for success, gotten razor-sharp at identifying the right opportunities, and leveled up your delegation process and communication skills.

But no matter how dialed in your delegation game is, you're still going to run into obstacles. Barriers. Roadblocks. Call them what you will, but they're coming for you.

CHAPTER 5: DIAGNOSING DELEGATION FAILURES

Maybe it's your deep-seated struggles with control and trust. Perhaps it's niggling doubts about your team's skills and capabilities. Or, maybe it's office politics and organizational inertia working against you.

Whatever form these barriers take, they can quickly turn even the most meticulous delegation efforts into a flaming dumpster fire if you're not careful. We're talking broken processes, a disappointing lack of accountability, and a whole bunch of frustration and hurt feelings all around.

So it's time for a real soul search and self-interrogation: What is it that's holding you back from delegation success? What fears and insecurities keep you firmly glued to the role of a control freak? Why do you keep butting heads with your team or spinning your wheels rather than leveraging their skills?

The hardest barriers to overcome are often the ones we create ourselves. The unconscious habits, mindsets, and behaviors that actively undermine the accountability-based environment required for delegation to thrive.

For many leaders, it all traces back to a lack of trust and confidence. Maybe you're haunted by nightmares of delegation disasters past, where a dropped ball led to public embarrassment or serious consequences. Or perhaps you just don't have enough data points yet to feel assured that your people are up to the task.

Others struggle with letting go and relinquishing control, fueled by intrinsic beliefs that they're the only ones who can do things "the right way." You know, that feeling of dread when you hand off an important task, coupled with delusional fantasies about how you'll swoop in like a superhero at the last minute to save the day.

When it comes to delegation going sideways, the buck stops with you as the leader—no ifs, ands, or buts about it. You can try to pass the blame or point fingers all you want, but at the end of the day, any major delegation failure traces directly back to you. Harsh? Maybe. But that's the burden of leadership.

From my experience, most delegation disasters tend to fall into one of three main buckets. Call them the three deadly sins of delegation, if you will.

The first deadly sin is **abdication**—as in, you stepped way too far back and abdicated your leadership responsibilities altogether. Maybe you put the wrong people in charge of the wrong things, essentially setting them up for failure before they even started. Or perhaps you gave someone a level of autonomy and authority that was wildly out of sync with where they were at in their professional growth journey.

Either way, abdicating your leadership responsibilities is a sure-fire way to turn even the most well-intentioned delegation scenario into a total laughingstock. You're the quarterback here, not some disinterested spectator. If you start chucking the ball randomly without a strategy, don't be surprised when the other team runs it back for six over and over again.

The second deadly sin that can shipwreck your delegation efforts? **Obfuscation**. That means you did a poor job of properly framing the task, articulating the vision of success, and providing the full context and guard rails for your delegates to operate within.

If you're vague with your communication, set unclear or unrealistic expectations, or fail to establish a robust system of accountability from the jump, then you're essentially setting everyone up to fail through an obfuscated mess of confusion and misalignment. It's delegation malpractice at its worst.

And the third deadly sin that can straight up murder your delegation dreams? **Suffocation**. You simply couldn't keep your inner control freak in check and felt compelled to incessantly micromanage every little detail along the way. Nothing saps motivation and disempowers people quite like having their leader constantly looking over their shoulder and second-guessing every move.

CHAPTER 5: DIAGNOSING DELEGATION FAILURES

If you think you might be falling back into suffocating micromanagement habits, do yourself a favor—ask your team point blank, "Am I over-managing you right now?" Best believe they're going to tell you. And their response will likely be something along the lines of "Well since you asked so nicely..."

The antidote? Intentionally take a huge step back and resist the urge to swoop in and fix every little perceived misstep. Trust that you've provided the proper framing, set clear expectations, and brought on board the right people for the job. Then get the hell out of the way and give your delegates the autonomy to spread their wings.

Whatever form your roadblock takes, the result is the same: delegation gets harder than it needs to be. Frustrations mount, confidence erodes, and you're left wondering why your supposedly high-performing team can't seem to get out of their own way.

So it's time to get radically honest with yourself. To dig deep and identify the root causes of what's really keeping you and your team stuck in delegation purgatory.

Here are some gut-punch reflection questions to get you started:

1. Which aspects of your delegation process are currently working well, and which areas need revision? Be brutally honest — don't hold back.
2. What about your leadership has ultimately led to the results (good or bad) that you're seeing?
3. Knowing what you know now, what would you do differently?
4. If you could somehow wave a magic wand and instantly eliminate the biggest barriers standing in your way, what would that unlock or make possible?

The answers to those questions may sting a bit, but that discomfort is par for the course when you're truly leveling up as a leader. Delegation mastery requires vulnerability and a willingness to look inward at least as much as it demands the right people and processes.

Have some tough conversations—with yourself, with your team members, and maybe even with others in the organization whose behaviors and dynamics are actively undermining your delegation mojo. It won't be easy or comfortable, but when has it ever been?

Whether it's a mindset shift to build more trust and release control, doubling down on clearer communication and expectation-setting, or doing the relational cha-cha to work through dysfunctional team dynamics, you've got to be willing to do the work to dismantle those barriers piece by piece.

And along the way, it's critical that you lead by example—walking the talk of accountability and delivery. You can't expect your team to push past their hang-ups and stumbling blocks if you're not modeling that same self-determination yourself.

So it's time for some honest self-coaching. Embrace the struggle and roll with the punches when delegation doesn't go as planned. Trust that your team's skills and commitment will grow over time as you persist (assuming you've put in the work to set them up with the right environment, expectations, and support).

Most importantly, keep your eye on the prize: a team running on empowered autonomy and accountability, where delegation is simply how work gets done. Make that the lodestar that guides you as you navigate obstacles and push past the barriers that have been holding you back.

These barriers don't have to be permanent roadblocks. View them as hurdles to overcome, as signals to pause and recalibrate. Revisit the five steps of delegation, plug the gaps, and stay the course. Trust the process.

Eventually, you'll reach that light at the end of the tunnel where empowerment replaces chaos, ownership replaces bottlenecks, and

CHAPTER 5: DIAGNOSING DELEGATION FAILURES

delegation replaces any semblance of the bad habits that may have held you back.

7

Chapter 6: Developing Your Team through Delegation

Here's where we take delegation to the next level by using it as a powerful tool for developing your team's skills and capabilities. You'll learn how to turn delegated tasks into coaching and growth opportunities. We'll also explore ways to celebrate successes (because positive reinforcement is key) and extract valuable lessons from failures. Get ready to invest in your team and reap the rewards of a highly-skilled, kick-ass workforce.

If you're a leader worth your salt, your single biggest responsibility isn't hitting some arbitrary revenue target or drafting a new corporate mission statement filled with MBA word salad.

No, your most important job as a leader is to be the steward of your team's talent. To identify those individual sparks of potential, to nurture them into roaring flames of capability, and to strategically deploy those skilled professionals in a way that maximizes their impact.

CHAPTER 6: DEVELOPING YOUR TEAM THROUGH DELEGATION

Anything less and you're just squandering one of the most precious resources you've got at your disposal. It'd be like owning a powerful sports car but choosing to leave it collecting dust in the garage rather than taking it out for laps on the open road.

That's why effective delegation isn't just a tool for offloading tasks or lightening your workload. No, delegation is a key vehicle for actively developing the skills, autonomy, and leadership capabilities of your team.

It's about discovering those latent leadership qualities in each person. It's about stretching and challenging them through thoughtful delegation of new responsibilities. And ultimately, it's about deploying those well-equipped individuals to have an even bigger impact.

I give you the three D's of delegation for development: **Discover**, **Develop**, and **Deploy**. Rinse and repeat that cycle over and over, and you'll build an unstoppable force of humble, hungry, and highly capable leaders at all levels of your organization.

But of course, that's much easier said than done. Developing your team's talents through delegation takes work. It requires keen judgment about where someone is in their growth journey and what's the right "next step" challenge to throw their way.

Too big a leap in responsibility, and you'll watch in horror as they flail and drown in a tide of overly ambitious tasks. Too small an increase in scope, and you'll suffocate their hunger for bigger challenges and opportunities to grow.

So as you kick off this journey of viewing delegation as a powerful development tool, start by asking yourself three key questions about each team member:

1. How fast can they learn and adapt to new challenges? What's their capacity for acquiring new skills?
2. How much can they take on before hitting their breaking point?

How can you "stack the logs" of increasing responsibility without going overboard?
3. What do they consistently give to those around them? Are they someone who uplifts others, or are they still individual players?

The answers to those questions will help calibrate your approach and lay the groundwork for tailoring your development efforts accordingly.

For those with clear leadership potential but relatively lower experience levels, delegation might mean stepping them through more fundamental "delegation 101" tasks with ample coaching and guidance. Baby steps at first, but stacking on more autonomy as their competence grows.

For your more seasoned professionals, it could be more about throwing legitimately big, hairy, audacious challenges at them and giving them the air cover to run with it. Less helicopter management, more championing from the sidelines with well-timed advice.

And for those members of your team who have the expertise but might be hitting a plateau or getting complacent? You'll want to use delegation to purposefully put them in new contexts—stretch roles that get them out of their comfort zones and unlock a fresh new level of growth.

Regardless of what development stage someone is at, effective delegation isn't something that happens in a vacuum. As you've figured out by now, you can't just toss tasks willy-nilly and expect growth to happen organically.

It requires intentionality in how you frame the opportunity, structure, and expectations, and above all, coach and support your delegates along the way.

That means formalizing delegation as part of a consistent coaching process and cadence. This should look like weekly 1-on-1 meetings, half an hour to an hour long, with each of your direct reports (and

CHAPTER 6: DEVELOPING YOUR TEAM THROUGH DELEGATION

preferably, encourage them to do the same with their teams).

These shouldn't just be boring "what happened this week" update meetings. You'll want to structure them as coaching sessions centered around each individual's current delegation projects and growth opportunities.

Use that quality time together to dig into their progress with open-ended questions like:

- What's the goal you're working towards here?
- What are your current options for tackling this project?
- What do you need to be at your absolute best right now?
- What needs to happen for this to be a successful outcome?
- What do you think the next steps should be?
- What aspects of our work could we start, stop, or keep doing?
- Is this your very best work?

See what I mean? You're not there to rehearse the play-by-play. You're a coach and a mentor, armed with just the right questions to get the best out of your delegates.

Does that mean you'll never advise, give directives, or course-correct when they stray wildly off track? Of course not—that's still a key part of your role as their leader and guide.

But the coaching framework should be the driving force in your approach. Resist the temptation to habitually swoop in and solve every little problem for them. Ask questions to untangle their thought processes and help them strengthen their critical thinking and decision-making muscles.

You're cultivating self-reliant leaders in their own right here, after all. So your value-add should primarily be pushing them with thoughtful prompts and creating the space for them to wrestle with challenges on their own.

Will it take more time and patience compared to giving them all the answers? Sure it will. As with delegation, coaching isn't about taking the easy shortcuts—it's about the long game of building autonomous capability.

Mind you, your work isn't done when the task is complete either. Here's where you introduce the *Success Log*. Whether it's at the end of a major delegated project as part of an after-action review or just a regular refresh on a quarterly or yearly cadence, have your delegate reflect on a few simple but insightful questions:

1. What were 3 things you crushed this time around? Lay out those little wins and accomplishments for the world to bask in.
2. What's one area or capability where you know you've got some growing to do? Self-awareness is a superpower.
3. Based on that self-identified growth area, what's one specific action step you can commit to taking to help make that improvement happen?

For your delegates, it's an incredible opportunity to flex those self-reflective muscles and consciously think through what's going well, what needs work, and how to keep pushing toward that next level of excellence. You're making personal growth an explicit part of the delegation process rather than just a hopeful by-product.

Plus, by actually documenting and tracking those responses over time in your trusty Success Log, you can monitor development trajectories, extract common themes that might warrant targeted training investments, and honestly assess whether you're striking the right balance between autonomy and hands-on enablement for each individual.

You're creating a straightforward and systematic way to document key lessons learned, acknowledge awesomeness, and map out future development priorities—all in one fell swoop.

CHAPTER 6: DEVELOPING YOUR TEAM THROUGH DELEGATION

I know, it all sounds like a lot. But any short-term pain or friction you experience will be worth it. Because you're not just getting immediate work delivered when you delegate with a development mindset. You're future-proofing your team with a deeper bench of skilled leaders ready to step up and take on bigger challenges.

You're paying it forward in a very real way by making your role more scalable and distributing empowerment throughout your organization. And perhaps most importantly, you're actively shaping your leadership legacy by grooming successive waves of impressive talent.

Be relentless in asking those thought-provoking questions. Resist the impulse to reflexively jump in with all the answers. Foster an environment of accountability and tough love where you have each other's best interests at heart.

There will be stumbles, there will be moments where your delegates fall fruitlessly on their faces in ways that make you wince. But those are the seeds of true growth and development. Let them happen, be there as a sounding board and guide, and watch as your talented team members rise stronger and more capable after every setback.

Before you know it, your thoughtful delegation and coaching will have paid off in the form of a veritable legion of next-in-line leaders ready and able to take your organization to new heights. That'll be the professional legacy you'll be most proud to leave behind.

So what are you waiting for? The development dojo is now in session—let's get coaching!

8

Chapter 7: Measuring the Impact of Delegation

You've put in the hard work to become a delegation rockstar, but how do you know if it's paying off? Here's where we'll explore ways to evaluate the effectiveness of your delegation efforts and track key metrics like productivity and performance. You'll learn how to gather data, analyze results, and continuously refine your approach for maximum impact. Time to prove that your delegation skills are worth their weight in gold.

Metrics. The very word might make some of you break out in a cold sweat of quantitative dread. But for those looking to truly master the art of delegation, having a strong grip on measurement is crucial. I'm not talking about slapping some graphs on a PowerPoint slide and calling it a day, either.

Let's start with the team side of the equation. Ideally, if you've gone through the process of framing delegated work properly by articulating

CHAPTER 7: MEASURING THE IMPACT OF DELEGATION

the description, rationale, parameters, and vision of success, then the actual task-level metrics should be pretty darn clear. We're talking quantifiable targets, deadlines, and delivery milestones that can be tracked without too much fuss.

But to gauge impact, you need to start looking at high-level business **outcomes**.

See, teams and individuals will naturally optimize for whatever specific numbers or targets you decide to measure and track. It's an unavoidable psychological force. If your sole focus is on "time to complete" and "on budget," well, you'd better believe your team will start hyper-optimizing for those narrow objectives at the expense of everything else—including quality, comprehensiveness, and impact.

The key here is to spend quality time upfront aligning with your team on defining clear desired outcomes and a mutually agreed upon vision of what genuine success looks like for the delegated workstream.

Is it revenue or efficiency targets you're after? Customer satisfaction scores or demonstrable skills growth for the delegates themselves? Whatever it is, get hyper-focused on distilling those large-scale impacts into quantifiable key results you can consistently measure progress against.

From there, you can work backward to determine the interim milestones, leading indicators, and progress metrics that'll act as legitimate bellwethers for whether your delegates are truly moving the needle toward those lofty outcome goals.

For example: instead of just counting task completions or output numbers, maybe you track user adoption and engagement funnels for a new product or service your dev team is building. Or maybe pipeline value, sales cycle velocity, and customer referral rates become the interim progress trackers for some delegated revenue accountability.

The key here is forcing your focus up to that outcome level rather than down in the process weeds. Teams will naturally shift their energy and efforts toward whatever measurements you collectively decide to emphasize. So if you make those measurements about high-impact business results and progress metrics, that's where their unbridled excellence and creativity will get channeled.

Focus on the "what", and let them take care of the "how". It's a much healthier delegation dynamic, and it keeps everyone's eyes on the bigger-picture prize.

Pair the data with some searching questions as you're scrutinizing your delegation impact:

- Are we truly pushing key ownership and autonomy down to the appropriate level of the organization?
- Do we have the right delegates in the right seats, or are we relying too heavily on small pockets of overachievers?
- What systemic bottlenecks or roadblocks are still gumming up the delegation machine, and how can we proactively remove them?

Take the time for those clarifying gut checks, then pair them with the right metrics, and suddenly you'll gain incredible insight into whether your delegation efforts are bearing genuine fruit.

If you've learned to implement the after-action review we talked about in the last chapter, you would have created a supportive space for you and your team to deconstruct successes and failures with total honesty. And perhaps most importantly, you ensure there's a clear mechanism for translating those learnings into decisive action by refining and optimizing your overall delegation model.

So build that habit of aggregating lessons learned and extracting key insights after every major delegation cycle. Schedule checkpoints with your most important people to reflect on what worked well, what broke down, and where your processes and capabilities still have room for improvement.

CHAPTER 7: MEASURING THE IMPACT OF DELEGATION

Of course, even with that crystal clarity around delegated outcomes and progress tracking, you can't forget about the other side of the coin: you as the leader and manager. What should you be focused on?

The single most vital variable in delegation success, what Jim Collins calls the number one metric, is simply this: "the percentage of key seats on the bus filled with the **right people** for those seats."

In other words, it's the who does what portion of the delegation equation—having the right personnel in the right roles. Take a page from Anne Mulcahy's book, and try to make your bus a "sparkling pocket of greatness". It's all about intensely focusing your energy and enabling a small cadre of rockstar talent you have full confidence in.

Make a clear-eyed assessment: How fully staffed and skilled is your personal delegation dream team? You need to determine whether your roster is stocked for sustainable outcomes. That last part is vital—delegation is a long game, so you have to maintain a sustainable talent pipeline to keep feeding it.

These two measurement threads together—crystal clear outcome tracking for your team's delegated work, paired with regular evaluation and bolstering of personal roster strength—these are the metrics that matter. It's quantifying the collective output while never losing sight of the human elements that make it all possible in the first place. Always remember that delegation success on an epic scale stems from focusing intently on people and outcomes first—not mindless box-checking and busywork.

Do that, and you'll have created the ultimate competitive advantage: a well-functioning team fueled by the perfect combination of talent and accountability.

9

Conclusion

Phew! If you've made it all the way to this conclusion, it means you've gone through all the blood, sweat, and tears to become a delegation master. Give yourself a pat on the back—you've earned it.

But before you go celebrating with a round of shots (or kombucha, if that's more your vibe), let's recap the key takeaways one last time:

First and foremost, delegation isn't just a luxury for managers—it's an essential skill that can quite literally make or break your success. When you delegate effectively, you free up your time and mental bandwidth to focus on the bigger picture stuff that matters. Plus, you empower your team to step up, take ownership, and develop new skills along the way. It's a total win-win.

Of course, mastering delegation isn't as simple as snapping your fingers and making tasks disappear. It takes careful preparation, clear communication, and a whole lot of trust-building. But now you've got the tools and strategies to tackle it head-on, from identifying the right opportunities to delegate to overcoming your control-freak tendencies to nurturing a delegation-friendly culture.

You've also learned some seriously powerful techniques to use

CONCLUSION

delegation as a development tool for your best employees. With these skills in your back pocket, you're ready to take on any delegation challenge that comes your way.

But most importantly, you understand that delegation isn't just a collection of tactics—it's a fundamental shift in your approach to leadership. It's about letting go, trusting your team, and empowering others to shine. It's about recognizing that you can't (and shouldn't try to) do everything yourself.

So, as you move forward in your management journey, remember to embrace delegation as not just a tool, but a mindset. Keep finding opportunities to hand over responsibilities, keep coaching and developing your team, and keep measuring your impact to refine your approach.

You've got this, delegation dynamo. Now get out there and start empowering your team to new heights of awesomeness!

www.ingramcontent.com/pod-product-compliance
Lightning Source LLC
Chambersburg PA
CBHW050248230526
45470CB00005B/2168